The Glass

An Ekphrastic Journey into Poetry, art, and Photography

Nix Moretta

© 2022

ISBN: 9798768460778

Published by Bold Ventures, Isle of Arran, Scotland, 2022.

Contents

The Glass Poet: The Art of Photography and Ekphrastic Poetry

Nix Moretta

Introduction

Visual and textual art forms do not reside in isolation[1]. When we observe a piece of art, or read a poem, we immediately feel a response to such, good, or bad. And this assessment forms a judgement, a critique, an analysis, a statement, a feeling, an experience. It affords a stimuli, whether we are thinking about the art of *Banksy, Tracey Emin, Rubens,* or *Matisse.* Similarly, via the texts of *Shelley, Keats, Byron, Wordsworth*, and *Eliot.* They all give us something. Even if at the time, we are

---

[1] *There is much debate as what actually constitutes art and literature, and such can be discovered further here:* *https://www.eolss.net/sample-chapters/C04/E6-87-02-04.pdf*

unaware of such, art matters.

Without, however, wishing to present this introduction as too 'academic,' (although, my ongoing studies enabled me to relish such, of which, I adore). I do feel it is important, and relevant, to give the reader some supporting evidence. Therefore, a non-comprehensive selection of notes and references for further reading, will be given to support my commentaries. However, as with all my texts, the final evaluation rests at your door.

I was raised in a working-class, Northern household, and spent time on my Great Aunt's dairy farm, (my halcyon days amongst animals, and within nature) where art was presented, and often discussed, as for the elite, not for country folk. Destined for the upper classes who had portraits of long dead relatives hanging in magnificent houses – and yet I was still interested in the arts. And consequently, painting, and literature, were my creative outlets from a young age. I would often be found painting flora, fauna, or wildlife. Or up playing the old piano; reading a book, or tapping away on my typewriter, playing with the art of text.

However, it was not until many years later, that I began to write poetry, as I had been inspired and influenced by the classics, particularly, the First World War poets, *Owen, Sassoon,* and *Brooke*, whom I am sure many of you will be familiar with. I could relate to their suffering and trauma, (although obviously I was not there, and not wishing to undermine the horrors they experienced) as I too had witnessed oppressively traumatic, emotive, and life-changing situations, never to be repeated. So, I wrote in an attempt to 'heal,' (in whatever format healing takes, and such is questioned in debate) to process, even at the time, I had no idea why, I just did. And I kept on writing, even through my seemingly darkest days.

And then, when I was fortunate, (and believe me, this was a struggle, because I was technically homeless at the time, and having to take on all manner of jobs, just to pay for my fees!) to study for my MA in Creative Writing nearing the age of fifty. Nearly thirty years after my undergraduate days in Cambridge. It was then I truly began to value the arts in all its many forms, and observe such through a different lens. 'Art for Art's Sake,' or, 'Le Pour l'art.'[2]

Creatively and therapeutically, art helps[3]. As it did for me as a child, escaping from the bleakness of the world. Art benefits our intellectual capacity, it strengthens our knowledge of the creation around us, and it reimburses our understanding of who, and what we are. Equally, my

---

[2] *Art for Art's Sake, often heralded by Oscar Wilde and his take on art being perceived as it stands, as it is, without moral, religious, cultural, social, political, or historic ideology. For more information, please see: https://www.jstor.org/stable/25587887?seq=1#metadata_info_tab_contents*

https://www.jstor.org/stable/40402974?seq=1

[3] *There has been extensive research undertaken into the therapeutic merits of the arts. Discussions of such can be entertained here for you to make up your own assumptions: https://www.alaindebotton.com/art/*

https://www.gilliebolton.com/

writing supports my mental health and well-being, it permits me to process situations, trauma, and relieves the stress of life in general. Just like many would maybe use a negative coping mechanism. Which are so symptomatic; by way of addictions, and dependencies, (and believe me, we all have them). These exist in various guises; food, alcohol, drugs, sex, violence, shopping, exercising, gambling, control, money, and work[4]. Yet when we look inwards, and embark on our journeys of serious internal work, (Jung, 1875 - 1961[5]) we begin to value our position, our genuine and authentic self of selves. To discern and decipher, what makes us truly inwardly content, and at peace. It cannot always be gleaned through

---

[4] *More on negative coping mechanisms can be found here:* **https://www.mentalhealth.org.uk/sites/default/files/stress-are-we-coping.pdf**

[5] *Carl Jung discusses at length, the inner work, archetypes, our shadow, introspection, and self-analysis, of which I studied extensively myself when I trained as a therapist and have been an analysand myself. More information on Jung and his amazing* *work:* **https://www.theguardian.com/commentisfree/belief/2011/may/30/carl-jung-ego-self**

https://www.oxfordreference.com/view/10.1093/oi/authority.20110803100027254

the bottom of a wine glass, or that next hit of heroin – they are just superficial and temporary aids that serve no one – the emotional pain still resides inside[6].

Visual art purports to my mental well-being too. Whether we create or enjoy other peoples' artistic meanders. There is a consensus, that we love museums, art galleries, exhibitions, and installations. It both unites and divides, yet rouses the appetite nonetheless – this is healthy, it is a known fact. For example, look at the growth of mindfulness, mandala colouring books for adults and children, art therapy, play therapy, meditation, yoga, talking therapies. These are not new phenomena, but almost like a return to the innocence of the child. We are therefore 'allowing'

---

[6] *Trauma and inner emotional pain are indicative of so many areas of debate and discussion. For more information, please visit:* ***https://www.louisehay.com/healing-ptsd-trauma-mind-body-anxiety/***

https://www.ncbi.nlm.nih.gov/pmc/articles/PMC3856773/

ourselves to be creative, and play, or to experience the notion of such[7].

The beauty of creativity is that it is so positive for us to embrace in our lives in whatever medium. The naivety of play we once embraced in childhood[8], needs to be rekindled. Therein, lies the rub of this book. It brings the visual world of photography, poetic prompts, and the arts together with the textual. It is about sanctioning the time, and space to be in nature, walking, and taking photos, and just being in that unknowing moment, when nothing else really matters. It is an encounter, a feeling, a wrath of emotive immersion. Creating value for the poet, reader, and observer – a reversion to that childhood pleasure of just being, and residing in the now, and it is rather bloody spectacular, the

---

[7] *The growth of the 'mindfulness' industry:* *https://www.theguardian.com/lifeandstyle/2019/jun/14/the-mindfulness-conspiracy-capitalist-spirituality*

[8] *Children, play, adults, learning, and innocence:* *https://core.ac.uk/reader/206240620*

feeling that is, not necessarily the book! (That's for you to assess!)

When I write, or take photos; paint, or read, I feel a plethora of emotions. From frustrations to euphoria. The process alone matters, not just whether I have written enough poems - or captured the 'right' image, not just about the academic world, or productivity, (for some, anyway) but how it makes us *feel*.

Equally, I love being in nature, and the outdoors. I love that semblance of peace we can garner from simple things. Even more so for many, as I write this during the global coronavirus pandemic spilling over into 2021 and beyond to 2022 - where people are taking to walking, and living more outdoors as a retreat from their lives cooped up inside. It's almost like a reset button, and that is what this book infers.

However, I have not arrived here alone. This book is a collaboration between the New Zealand photographer and artist, Andrew Collins, (the creator of my book cover. Links to his work to the rear of this book.) Such was born out of that love of the arts, photography, nature, play, innocence, creativity, being in that sacred moment; and literature. A union, a manifestation of muses and inspiration, one helping the other, and vice versa. And it was via Andrew's artistic presentations through his work and photography, that I began to think about things differently. How I could begin, again, to appreciate what I had always loved, but had hidden or denied. And similarly, how we bounced off one another, creatively, mutually respectful of each other's work.

It also concerns my move to Scotland, which was totally cathartic for me. To allow myself to exist in a location that would serve my soul far from the madding crowd. Somewhere remote, and hard to reach, to be immersed in nature, where I could dedicate more of my time to doing what I love, writing, (but also having to work to pay the bills like we all do!) and taking photographs on my travels. All the photographic (with some personal print and paint-based insertions) art is my own, (except Andrew's where mentioned.) I am a complete amateur, and make no judgement on artistic style or merit. However, I am learning and experimenting with respect to what I wish to convey, equally mirrored by the text.

So, I would love you to enjoy this book as both a poetic exploration into the ekphrastic world[9], and how we can be inspired to write or think about the arts and photography, and what they mean to us, especially during highly challenging times.

Think of such as a reset button for yourselves in your daily worlds, a time out. Likewise, for me, as a poet, and a mental well-being warrior, something that has facilitated my own personal development,

---

[9] *Ekphrastic elements of writing about art through poetic means, can be explored further here:* https://www.poetryfoundation.org/learn/glossary-terms/ekphrasis *(Although some may say I am not technically responding to art, I am inspired to write a poetic response to an art form, not seemingly obviously connected to that photograph, but how it makes me 'feel.')*

and healing, of which, I believe, needs to be shared.

I hope you enjoy.

Blessings and light.

Nix Moretta, Scotland, 2022.

Poet's Biography

The Lancastrian born poet, Nix Moretta, a survivor, and thriver, of trauma, abuse, homelessness, poverty, an eating disorder, and mental ill health, has written poetry since a young age.

By her own admission, Nix left home at the age of fifteen with nothing. Nix suffered, with time spent in asylums, due to many failed suicide attempts; and was pimped out as a sex worker to survive on the streets as a teenager.

However, with hope and a stoic sense of determination, she went back to school, and graduated from university against all odds. As a result, Nix went on to work for the Civil Service, including teaching in prisons, and lecturing at Cambridge University.

Moreover, Nix experienced careers in equestrianism, owning and running riding schools; retraining former racehorses, (which formed the base of her equine science doctoral studies) and organic farming.

Nix has supported environmental concerns, and maintained, and advocated for traditional farming methods, and managing rare breeds. As a vegetarian, however, Nix utilised the animals, in their therapeutic sense. Subsequently, amassing a menagerie of unwanted farm animals to help traumatised children, and young adults, through their own journeys of self-discovery.

Sadly, the mental ill health remained, and after a nervous breakdown in her forties during her first PhD, Nix re-evaluated her life, and embarked upon an MA in Creative Writing. Such was completed in a caravan, on her farm during the first lockdown of 2020. It was here she birthed her first two books; revisiting material over thirty years' old, and creating a new body of work.

Nix now lives peacefully on the Scottish Isle of Arran running a Bed and Breakfast; writers' and artists' retreats, book clubs, and therapeutic creative writing workshops. She has two grown up children, and a grandchild. With a loving nod to her previous equine related existence, she is also accompanied by the first of her riding school ponies, a twenty-six-year-old, happily retired Mr. Fudge; a true spirit animal, and unicorn in training.

Staunchly non apologetic about her life, and work; authenticity, now, as a poet, and a free-spirited woman with a wonky brain, is paramount.

Madness is not a persecution.

This is her third book of poetry.

Dedication

This book is dedicated to the Island of Arran. You saved me with the gift of solitude, and recovery. I hope one day, I will be at peace.

Acknowledgements

Thanks must go to a plethora of Arran islanders, and her visitors, who have supported my poetic journey, and continue to inspire me. Immense thanks and gratitude go to my collaborator, the New Zealand artist and photographer, Andrew Collins, and the artist behind the book's cover.

Immense warm light-filled hugs must also go to Katie Lindsay-Brown of South Whittlieburn Farm, Largs, Scotland. You showed me how not to be fearful of life anymore, with your effervescent dynamism.

There are many people who have inspired me along my life's trail, (and trials!)and these have been duly mentioned in my other books. However, you have not been forgotten.

In addition, thanks go to my English professors, both at college, and all universities I have attended. Without their guidance and encouragement, I could not have continued.

Moreover, appreciation must go to the academic, and Royal Literary Fund fellow, Dr Sally Cline, and my creative writing lecturers, Dr Sophie Nicholls, and Dr Jenna Clake. You all helped to open my mind to new literary possibilities.

Equally, a posthumous thank you to the late Professor Petruska Clarkson, whom I once met in bizarre circumstances, yet she changed the way I thought about myself, and the world around me, forever.

To my readership, who follow my progress, understand my work, and buy my books; thank you for seeing my soul.

And finally, to my darling families in England and Scotland; my gorgeous children, Max and Poppy, and granddaughter, Orla.

I hope you truly comprehend why writing is my life blood. This is what I was born to do.

Thank you.

Nix Moretta, Scotland, 2022.

The Glass Poet: The Art of Photography and Ekphrastic Poetry

Portencross Pier, North Ayrshire, Scotland,

January 2021

1) The Aperture

Do not tell me how to live, for I am already dead.

Show me the aperture for love,

at the water's edge.

Comfort me in crimson glow and blanket me in
violent voices.

Crumble the shore and pebble the route to divine

Speckle the egg and plate up emotion.

Lock up the room and close all your doors.

Speak to the sun; whisper the moon.

Cry to the lark, and herald upon moors.

Courtyard Corridor, Amber Palace, Jaipur, Rajasthan,

Andrew Collins, 2018.

2) Restrictions

Choking viaduct dreamscape
Lens narrow capture void
Sidewalk, backstreet pin-up
Enrobing, cascading there

Greyscale, monolith empire
Screams of deathly pale
Whitewashed, rendered faceless
Fade to fake, milk stream

Playful, mindful seepage
Coloured in nature's way
Bondage, shouldered, gather turret
Window, ledge, to drop

Solo dying tree against a wintry sky, High Kildonan Forestry Road, Isle of Arran, 2022.

3) *Life*

Soiled and covert covens

Coddled by the pull

Of gravitational battery

Above to bomb

From hanging oak plinth spikes

Upon the wringing of the loch

As bodies thresh the air

To saucers of burnt repugnant

Stuffing pupils with witchcraft

Coloured in grey marl sweaters

Suffocated by the lens through a

glass less pale

Where the ash decays to fade

Windowpane, Andrew Collins, New Zealand, 2020.

4) *The Pain with a View*

He left me breathless

And his mist deluged

the wound

Where the carrion danced

And black cabs died

As a back door man

He felt like embers at my feet

Trickery, Macbethian air

Crackled pots

And wheels rioting

In breadcrumbed streets

He held my gnarly fingers

To a macabre tale

Of twisted ringlets

Greeta Falls, Largs, North Ayrshire, Scotland,

January, 2021

5) *To the Moor*

Bunk bed mountains

And duvet falls

Silent burns

And rutted cairns

To signs of air apparent

Where the blood cave severed

And teeth gnawed

Wooded parapets of soundless

Wails as the shoulders

Carried an army of

Cries in tourmaline moats

Sunset at Inverkip Bay, Scotland, January, 2021.

6) Inverkip Bay

When night evades all light

I had to let you go

As firebrands electrified the hearth

I sought sanctuary cold beneath

Where cotton showers hailed to colour

And silent moors muffled grey

As winter splinters on to spring

I found death to start again

Sitka Forest, Urie Loch Trail, Isle of Arran,

Winter 2021.

7) *The Burn*

Molten light seeps through

The gorse kissed earth

As sheep graze silently

And as the sun sits quiet

Upon the old glen's knee

The winter pines, dance wordlessly

The silver dapple grey hails to errant skies

And sorrows a mournful hymn

As Eastern winds sigh breathlessly

Kissing murmuring shores

The broods they whicker for fields of fire

And harriers chant the air

The midden steams with

Childlike glee

Padding to burn and byre

Escape the lark and trim the sea

Flail to arms and mock the call

Bank the wonder and plight armoury

Chinese Lakes, Brisbane Glen, North Ayrshire,

January, 2021.

8) Equinox / Equinox Dawn II / A Thousand Yard Editorial Stare

Return at once

To .

Pass all souls

That channelled the anchor fire

In a pit of hope

And pints of ale

By a h'penny hooker

And a barrage balloon

Weighted by the heart of your string

Cast out over the burn

Like mother's washing line

And the back yard lavvie

To

Capture a lament

Of the equinox dawn

Return at once

To

Pass all souls

That channelled the anchor engine fire

In a pit of hope and pints of ale

By a ha'penny hooker

And a barrage balloon

Weighted by the eitchen

Cast out over the scald

Selling matches by the docks

To gentlemen and grave robbers

Consuming

Metal gags - bullet metal airs

And Shelley's tales

To capture a lament

Where Lear froze at the juncture

On a road to knitting needle death

Suturing strychnine waists

Belted at the knuckle

As whalebone sighs

Dread the nought

Heavy whispered pain

Chest drawn quartered

As the solemn soldiers

Marched as butchered boughs to

Weighted wheelwrights blow

Glass horizons grey

Radiata Pine, Tauranga, New Zealand, Winter, 2020,

Andrew Collins.

9) *The Case of the Wooden Tree*

Formless editorials on elongated

Stained tea-cups

Void of leaves

Sing needles knots

Double backed to trident moulds above

Floundering

The universe impaled vacuous veins

Animas inherit all shadows

You held me through to morning rain

As mirage held below

Eas Mor Ecology, Kildonan, Isle of Arran,

September, 2021.

10) *The Quiet Man*

Somewhere

Silently

Hiding above canvas canopies of soft whorls indigo

where veins seep out to grieve

Love holds him captive timeless on the breeze

Bondaged as a flageolet

Weeping on both knees

Stranglehold of will in pain

Freedom binds his whisper

To begin again

Goat Fell at Brodick Bay, December 2021,

Isle of Arran.

11) *The Purple Rabbit and the Golden Leopard*

I wore my many hats today

And fluffed the peacock feathers

Fissured, fusillade, fanciful

They withered at the girdle

And as the breath wore close

I captivated pleasant

To iridium luminosities

Strangled, young, and svelte

She bound her many hates today

And stuffed the mangolds richer

Radiant, ruddied, rancid

They swallowed up bereft

Common grey seal at Skelmorlie, Western Scotland,

during high tide, January, 2021.

12) *The Seals of Skelmorlie*

Oh! to be a fat-grey skinned lay-about

Laughing at the shore

Juggling flippers rampantly

And knocking on herring's door

Barking at the tourists

Flaying at the rock

Camouflaged like pirates

Pulling up wet socks

Yet when the Sun God

Hastens fall, and winter takes a bow

The water nymphs snap stifle strict

And lure the grey mire depths

Ribboning the fire blue air; wrapping of the winds

Silver polishing creation; cradling those that
wept

Forestry Trees, Lamlash, near Dunn Ffion,

Isle of Arran,

Winter, 2021.

13) *The Fallen*

Blacken the hand that crawls to bed

And creeps the maiden's sheets

Syphoned windows and symphonies' applause

Murderous operandum

Kraken the depth gauge to plumb

Nautical miles set against tidal clocks

Pewter plastic needles silence the yarn

Synapses frontal to decay

Dead trees, Glenashdale Forestry, Whiting Bay,

Isle of Arran,

March, 2021.

14) *The Three Sisters*

Stood erect; silent, like a muffled burn waits for

winter rain. They projected to the sun, and rooted

to the earth. For their missile silo exeunt at the

cage and wept a sigh of a bough, and molten,

monogrammed skies cradled a rowdy day, where time

killed the light, and the forest

kissed the ocean pale.

Glen Rosa, Isle of Arran, Summer 2021.

15) *Lost*

I drew a black line one day and it followed me

home

Nipped at my heels and silenced my bones

Froze out my womb and sutured all holes

Cast nets and wildebeest loomed out the spoils

Dread naught and nothingness complete the poem

A Beach on Arran, Winter, 2022.

16) *The Wasters' Land*

Cosmic time abundant of all binds, where seascapes captivate the truth in you. Sit awhile and feel at peace, triumphant on the silver hearth.

Radiant and dead.

Moon the stone to mire the matter.

Enterprise and will.

Raptured, ruptured cornucopia murders

Rendered at the quiff.

Portencross Castle, North Ayrshire,

Winter 2020.

17) Black Ash

As black ash seeps from a silent shore, winds eke whispers from the west. Sun gods dance to dying light, and there, beside a mountain pass we exist amongst the ether, as cosmic prisms cast delinquent shadows, and my deathly love parts ways with yours.

Crippling stews of stoned ramparts of fire

Raging antiquities of pain.

Gripe the child on toothless whim.

Wind the ticket to a grotto of inns

And a copulate of wills.

Chunda on minutes of billows as sodden

Skins rub the fat and stars greed the night.

Arran hills from the String Road, Isle of Arran,

Winter, 2022.

18) *Arranian Monoliths*

Decorative armistice meddled

Worn and trench footed

Etched out the bells

Of lamentable skies

Weeping sunrises

On permeable lands

Hijacking turreted rooms

Where hands vault the glaze

And pipers night the depths

Kilmory Beach, Isle of Arran, Summer 2021.

19) *The Beach*

As swallows mantra airs

Oceans hymn below

Where sandstone

Paves to glass

And waves ink no more

Sirens tune the lute

Enveloping raconteurs

As cannon fires the red gun

Wastelands

Turrets massacre macabre in inchknots

Torrylinn Cairn, Kilmory, Isle of Arran,

Summer 2021.

20) *The Lost Poem of the Blue Mute*

Sandwiched at the wedge

Caliphdom fiefdom idiom rage

Modernist notation

Feminist dreamscape lands of nonsense

And postcard manuscripts where

A room with no tide

Sets sail by the piper

With winds red

Charm offensive

Readied with a militia

Of serpents

Front and vertebral

Inhaling inoculated airs

Glenashdale Falls, Isle of Arran, Spring 2021.

21) *Whip the Lash*

Synapses frontal to the waterways

Buttering skins on murderous airs

Time ticks the slate

Sound the course to mock and whorl

Greet them masters of descent of slumber

Pale skins on crumbled puddings

Catacomb the lair

Flock the pan and sift the chaff

Purulent wonder and fault split the neck

Embargoed pelts on potted ash

Squat faced prosaic

Bedizen the corpse pale the braid

Blackwaterfoot Beach, near the King's Caves, Isle of Arran, Winter 2022.

22) *White the Sea*

The sea she summoned to come ashore

Whilst the land ushered her to the depths

Where the sun escaped the firmament

The clouds they mocked to yield and wept

The sound did white the errant star

As invert aquilegias ebullient afoot

Where horizon clay warriors riled the jute

The pacifist rot requiem to *Achates*

Mill workings, Andrew Collins, New Zealand, 2019.

23) *The Calling*

The factory wept for children's fingers and looms

darkening paste coloured

walls as the women marched

to wash feather caps where the beams erupted in

plight

Men fought a war with words and ink spilt the mist

Streets were bound in shoelace filth and carpet

monochrome air

Gargoyles for graves and teapots as drunk as

stoves on

gaskets piped at dawn bleeding

Telegrams injected to black

Circamon and the Devil's Gate

Ink and gouache on canvas board.

Nix Moretta, Winter, 2021.

24) *Circamon and the Devil's Gate*

Swept up tapped raptor delight
Hidden lair back door trapped out of sight
Flageolet back pain wrapped around tight
Dog collar loose molar set the noose right

Bind the feet concubine walled spit to spite
Jug the hare bend the round bricked flit to flight
Bedroom mirror hand brush stroked banal plight
Inked pen plant pot pale yellow moon sprite

Oak tines timed rinds ocular respite
Cherry pinch ranch dressed secular bite
Window lead rib beam semantic erudite
Cadaver dread sapphire painted saprophyte

Kilpatrick Forestry, Isle of Arran, Spring, 2021.

25) *Pale the Light*

Stretcher the bow side stern

Looked the glass to the rim

As the cracked sought the cadaver

Tails the sorcerer blanched

Flexuous like the stain on the lead

Girdled and glaived to the imbrue

Limn lucidity cradled the mage

As the mephitic mere bled

The Bass Rock, between the King's Caves, and Blackwaterfoot, Winter 2022, Isle of Arran.

26) *The Black Line Sew*

Block me a wood of trauma blows

Blood let the sky

Winkle the creeper

And draw down the moon

Sunrise the leper

Melt the air mauve

Silence the wakening

And sew the word lipped

Largs harbour at dusk, North Ayrshire, Scotland,

Winter 2021.

27) *The Red Book*

The red book screamed like a fizzy can lid

Burst at the bark like a bank

Melted the ink and cast out the binds

Flared to the second-hand cart

Tongue tailed cattle press

Oxidised iron mongered still

Countenance faces etched

Cado's pleading in ruddy cheeks

Prologued minds mining firing blanks

Live the tor

Step on the aluminium rust

Clouds chide the curse

Verulam tears and

Handcrafted souls

In fielded rows

Undertaking the embalmer

Tipping the boot shine

Kneel to the line

The Red Book whinnied

Like castrated twine

Sand ripples, Isle of Arran, Winter 2022.

28) *Waves of Melancholia*

Hung like the badger

Trap whistle stop railway

Dying in the town where

Potatoes slice the grain

Incite to riches of headscarves and the noose

As crimped carcasses lay silent in gorse

Sea salt tender upon the hip

Patriarchal welts at the cummerbund

Imprinted hails on the crag sign bare

As the lighthouse laughed ensnared

Pillage the skies and rape the light

Sever the clouds and take down the rain

Stay awhile and rest your bones

On loch air glides and mountain pass

As paper trails to shore and glen

To falls and when triumphant

Blow air cheeks to mottled crimson

And shift the dead axe moor

Coventry Cathedral, England, UK, Summer 2020.

29) *Monochrome Scoundrel*

Monochrome scoundrel

Round the bends

Under the hairline

Crack to the wind

Green the trumpeter

Herald no sound

The soldiers come

Candle the window

Ocean the sigh

Diarised and rampant

Tyrant the window

Block fissured sight

Contour the light

On seven potions fair

Distemper the gaslight

Tied the red rope tight

Bed flaying oxygen

Trapped at the whine

Blackouts and stockings

Strangulate the air

Hungry and itching for

Thousand-yard stares

Blackwaterfoot Beach looking over to the Kintyre
Peninsula, Isle of Arran, Summer, 2021.

30) *July is Rising*

July is rising halt
The line of the pear
March orchard home
A mire in the making

Nescient noxious orbs
Bounce like the ether
Sit to poach the lair
A refulgent urgency

July is rising spare
The belt of the line
Roundelay the slumber
A refuge of decay

Beach combing, Argyll and Bute, Winter 2020.

31) Unclip

Sinews exit
From the front line of emerald
Grey marl trenches

Stuffing your eyes with plastic bags
From the compost heap coloured in ammonite
Suffocated by the lens through fractured repose
Where the ash decays to fade

Chain up your art and anchor the moon
Open the drawer to secrets and lists
Sequence a thought on ocular mist
To smudge the gate wired

Seamill Beach, North Ayrshire, Winter 2020.

32) *Tether the Art*

Anchor bound and rich to the hoary

Marching on to dawn

Where whispers catalogue the wails

And silence fumes the worn

Wearied stark and solitary

Armoury battle post

Stars to mock the gentile

Lights remain for ghosts

Bennecarrigan Free Church, (now closed) Isle of Arran, Winter, 2021.

33) *Subservient Existence*

Tourniquet a requiem of dreams

Held by the throat

Taut

Ligatures

By accidental

Stamps at the wrist

Lamping on monroes

Storm break the cherry

Paraffin the stove stone bothy crypt

Crept the spring

From winter born laments

Eas Mor Library, Isle of Arran, September 2021.

34) *Immaculate Incarcerated Lemons*

Impregnated lemons

Hanging from their sleeves

Wearing Sparks' pullovers

And fraying at the weave

Chewing over whist drives

Defecating dead

Hammock string on noose-dom

Frontline emerald trench

Grey lark for balloon whisks

Pith and pip do swell

Mountains for a lip seal

Lemon barks to dwell

Yellow is the colour

Fragrant on the turn

Toxic and triumphant

To the glass sojourn

Pebbles on Machrie Beach, Isle of Arran,

Summer 2021.

35) *By the Grit Bins*

Fulcrum plumblines and moniker glass

Dwellings hidden by the bankrupt air

Jubilant cries like babies in baskets

Abandoned at Lincoln Inn's gate

Women with washed out skins barrage their eyes

As the menfolk take the soap and the brush

Burning all the books and purple scarves whilst

Whipping them on to work

Seafoam, Andrew Collins, New Zealand,

Summer, 2020.

36) Seafoam

Tip where the light consumes the day

And amber pales the soul

As demons hail the blood of thieves

To wonder timeless

And conceive

Of native journeys onward

Ticketless

Halls

Of abandonment

Foiled the whip!

Suffocate the arm

Wrap the bend

Red the last

Cry unexamined seafoam

Mark making on cream pots

Dead diners washed in a tin bath

By a tinted glass fire

Suffocating skins

Barbed in muddied mink

Aspic in battered parchment

Tattooed arias four fours

Cloaked by the math

Arran coastal walk between Kildonan and Kilmory,

Isle of Arran, Autumn, 2021.

37) *Impale the Moon*

Leave a window ajar like a spinning top to the
universal lie

Sit by the stained church alter of liquid light

and all unknown shall be known

Tourniquet a chant of washed indigo nightshades

Held by the window latch

Snared by generals in the trench with puttied
ankles

Gnarly like starlings breached at birth

Wemyss Bay Clock Tower, Inverclyde, Scotland,

December, 2020.

38) Shall I Knit You

Shall I knit you a sweater with my blood

As my ribs clack the yarn

And the coal burns the eyes

Shall I pour you a mountain with my soul

As my mind feasts with anger

And the wood grinds the skies

Will you send me a letter stamped with tears

As your body tempers monologue

And the oil flays denies

Inverkip Boat House, Inverclyde, Western Scotland,

(with the Arran hills behind,) Winter 2020.

39) *Light not the Sea*

Fable me a light where dark reigns above

As Westerly kisses eke towards the 'orison

And pebble grey shores hurry to blushes

Of errant hope casting stale shadows

Upon an echoed sallow

Enable the drum, and cast out the dark

Herald cygnus buccinator amidst cosmic ether

Switch on the flow, seam the ache

Pastel the white, and mute the moon

Paint the subtle palette

Whisper an allegory of iridium joy

Where wily oaks mock the lark

And mourners fade

Multilayered and blanketed

Cosseted pulls of gravitational arcs

Call out the blue monologues

Upon lochs of radiant airs

Where pipers monarch the sight

Luminous and flushed in the forest

As paths forge the union to life

Where clouds are fat and wasted

Like mirrored halls of guttural quiet

Galvanised as toads in glass-bottomed boats

Abandoned books, Andrew Collins, New Zealand, Summer 2020.

40) *Poetry is the Narratology of the Soul*

Lacing faces in plastic bags tied at the wrist

Sounding like a whistle on the lantern stove

Driven by parallel lines in a sunken

glass canister

Holstered at the jaw-bone leash

Muted clouds formed by dead poets and

Conversations with anomalies

Where rivets kill the join

And text plumbs to regimental order

As chartered courses drag the weeping

Lexicons and semantic notions strangle the hold

Drowning with diction and dogma

Caught on the line in font and ash

Clambering ragged and drugged

Tyrannical and cleaved

Defecating spectral orbs of oiled remains

Yomping with buttered toast on arcs

Of fumigator energy

Murdering the embryonic tinned peach

Clothed in clotted yarn

Kildonan beach looking over to Pladda Lighthouse,

Summer, 2021.

41) *Kildonan*

Formless editorials on elongated stained teacups

Porcelain slain of chip

Void of leaves

From needles knots

Double backed to trident knolls

Urchins prick the souls and boulders chain the hip

Where the blue kills the void

And the island stares to knock

From sour-faced riptides

Tripping on seekers binds

Machrie Standing Stones, Isle of Arran,

Autumn, 2021.

42) *The Stones of Machrie*

She sits by inkwell of quill and mire

Where moons do banal and

Skies quake the dark

Sutured mountains thresh the skin

Where needles pine to arms

And burns quash the eye

Ir. No.77 noose the barrel drum

As mercurial life pans

And the blue cold steals the stole

Gourock, looking over to the Isle of Bute,

Winter, 2020.

43) *Tailor a Fox Brush*

Tailor a fox brush in fire glove white

Sandbox the glen rose to stone

Molten the lead kill the down stair

On uphill tangents to dread

Bleed me an ocean in scissored repose

As the mountains quell and wise

Speak the tongue to the tripwire

On fractured wooden barked cries

Cormorant on Kilmory Beach, Summer, 2021,

Isle of Arran.

44) *Willow and Pew /Dead Not the Wing*

Camber on a wing of light

Stapled where the tinctoria-black ire

Devours all air

As plastic dolls rest on

Fake railway sleepers

And uniform vests

String at the wilt

Somber me a songbird

Strangled at the lung

Where concrete trees axe

The blood-let pale

And wranglers toxify

Griddled

Wet plumes of choke

Saltwater spirits limp

By a golden goose egg

Noose

Knotted with the filament

Tilted at the turn

Where soot ash pale

Children on clog cobbles

Go hungry

Like mill town

Weavers

Cast the yarn

Through a lens

Upon mercurial

Pewter riddled streets

View to Holy Isle from the Ross Road, Lamlash,

Isle of Arran, Winter, 2021.

45) *The Town of Dhallol*

Human puddings of forty elements

Needing a battery

Sat erect as

Mercury, baked dry our

Spiritual coffees as

Europe, the ice moon, and

Galileo's dust, of 1610 sat in

Aura's wilderness measured by a

Micronic diameter eaten by

Surface crusts and raped by

Penetrative iron maidens

Piercing your organs as you lay in a

A geyser of ice

Oceanic like

Seismic caverns drenched in an

Avalanche of pulverised lava dancing in

Pyroclastic flow

Mouthing moments via a

Rift valley system

Flanked by

Fumaroles and

Potash

Camel caravans flayed by the

Liquefaction of life and

Mudflows of energies

Hydroelectric tears fell that Augustian day in

November

You gorged out the caerulean veined wall of water

with a reservoir of pain in a Vajiant dam

Consumed by C a S 0 4

Salt flats and

Solar winds swallowed stilettos as

Sirius a star in Orien's belt held

Telescopic monocled luddites and

Found a home in poetry led by

A pod of caterpillars dancing

La Passigiata towards

Scablands where you

Carved your signature in

Atmospheric pressure as

Gnostic gospels prayed to

Canyons of

Outflow channels captured in a

Anthemically crescendo drone through

Alleys and byways

Caught in swift air streams by the

Mars Rovers

The world is a scratch card

Flourishing

Life in chemistry

Coastal walk between Kings' Caves, and Blackwaterfoot, Isle of Arran, Winter, 2021.

46) Ars Poetica

Block the fissure of all light

Stop the hammer on the wall

Recede the ebbing of the flow

And mask the beating of the blood

Hole the whiting of the moor

Stitch the melting of the pain

Dye the colour slate to grey

And cry a salt night to the loch

Fight the journey onward seas

Poet a whisper presaged to dusk

Search for meaning halt all vision

Scream a mountain to the peak

Flay the spirit cease all time

Le pour de art a palette to fade

Forest the mud lark sing to axe

And born of winter death to mount

Brisbane Glen Road, near Largs, Western Scotland,

Winter 2021.

47) Dawn of the Obsidian

The ribbon straw boater

Lairs the wordless way

As troubles stone the thoughts

And mountains creep to night

Jet the light

Stripe the dawn

Desk the mirror

And flog the sea

Mind the minded

Curtain no dusk

Carpet the window and

Bolt the line

Rounded circumnavigated they came

Cyclical narrators stuck in the lobotomies scalpel

Sucked out the silicone breast

Cupped and cut from the optical bare

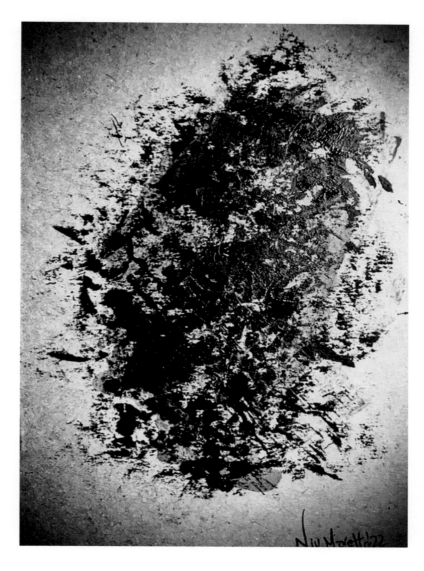

Author's own copper block print painting,

'Breakdown,' Ink on board

48) Text in Orbit/Frontal Lobal Lyrics/Breakdown

Do not judge me on the aesthetic

Or the historic

Histrionics

Empathetic

Lethargic

Or whether I'm egocentric, are you?

Hah!

Is it plutonic

Ironic

Is she psychiatric?

Who's asking who!

Neurotic

Anthropocentric

Do we reside in

Sub atmospheric?

Does your mind think

Eccentric

Electric?

Rhetoric

Esoteric

Barbaric?

Do not judge me on the

Generic

Semantic

Subtopic

Heliocentric

Deficit

Kilmory beach at sunset, Isle of Arran,

Summer 2021.

49) *Burnt Umber*

Straddle the light

Darken the palette

Hail to the Sun Gods

The autumn pales

Beckon the weeping

Abandon the summer

Call out to sirens

The ocean wails

Mother's Shed, Andrew Collins, Tauranga, New Zealand, Summer 2020.

50) *The Poet*

Conscripted compartmentalised dogmatic rust

Rounded white and battle weary

Percolated trusts

Where paperless trees held typewriter keys

And blood ink ribbon strangled lead

Wrist bound dead

Heathen like a breeze

String backed whiplashed rope burn bed

Where dying monoliths captured

Rudimentary greens on earth shires

Filed with staples at the hinge

Where the cracked lead tabernacle dropped anvil

dust

Residing in the ether trope

Where skies part ways with the light

Eternal sunrises evaporate in poetic

Rowdy guides filled with hope

References

For more information on ekphrastic poetry, and poetry in general:

www.poetryfoundation.org

www.poets.org

www.poetrysociety.org.uk

www.poetryarchive.org

www.poems.com

www.poets.org

www.nationalpoetryday.co.uk

Links

(As of Winter, 2021)

For public speaking, poetry recitals, workshops, tuition, and media information, please email:

nixmorettapoet@gmail.com

For more details on Nix's life and work, please visit:

www.nix-moretta.co.uk

To purchase my photographic poetry cards:

www.etsy.com/uk/shop/PoeticPhotoCards

YouTube channel: **Nix Moretta**

Instagram:

@theglasspoet

@nixmorettapoet

@thearranpoet

To listen to free audio readings and lectures:

soundcloud.com/nix-moretta

For information on my photographic collaborator, Andrew Collins, and the designer of the book cover, please see:

@andrewcollinsphotography

facebook.com/tomasfarrowartist/

Disclaimer

Nix Moretta is not a clinician, or medical professional of any kind. Her background is predominantly academia, and is currently working towards a PhD in Literature.

Any advice and commentary given within is purely subjective, yet researched, nonetheless. The approach to the therapeutic qualities of the arts in all its forms, is well documented via the links and references presented.

The reader is tasked to be mindful of any triggers which may occur upon reading, or viewing the photography, and to seek support from trained professionals where necessary.

However, the author has worked extensively within education and therapeutic environments, and successfully facilitated writing groups for a diverse range of people.

This book, therefore, is a quiet performance of the author's own creative, and mindfulness regime, which has aided her own mental well-being.

Endnotes

I do not consider myself to be a photographer, nor do I necessarily wish to be viewed as one. My photos are either taken with an Apple smartphone, or a Kodak digital camera with a Vanguard tripod.

Photography really began for me during lockdown in 2020, when I moved to Scotland, as I was encouraged to do so by Andrew Collins.

The inspiration to capture those moments through the lens, is not one born out of ease. I believed previously, those private flashes should not be held captive in photographic form, nor overly manufactured with filters, cropping, and composition.

However, just as I edited, chopped, tweaked, and honed my textual presentations here, I began to relish the equally therapeutic elements of playing with the photos, to add depth or otherwise. To play with the sense of play, just as this book aims to present, without removing elements of the organic, raw, unedited nature.

Moreover, the value of experimentation often becomes lost in adulthood, as we fill our days with 'stuff;' often seemingly worthless escapades into a life full of expectation.

(If you visit my YouTube channel, you will observe this idea further, when I discuss the parameters of poetic, artistic, and creative endeavours.)

This book, therefore, is not a manifestation of art, photography, poetry, and literature as many may possibly assess. Alternatively, positioned simply as a piece of creativity, which means everything to the author; hopefully resonating with the reader.

Ultimately, as I always mention in my book commentaries, the interpretation, via a contradiction to my previous statement; (which I feel I am permitted as a poet) remains with you. Everything to me is art, and art matters in all its forms.

Nix's fourth book of poetry will be released late 2022, early 2023, *'Equinox: Poems from the Blue Chair.'*

(Please note, semantical; grammatical alterations, and punctuation nuances are completely intentional.)

'She could have been a poet, or she could have been a fool.'

('This Night Has Opened My Eyes,' The Smiths: Morrissey and Marr, 'Hatful of Hollow,' 1984).

Printed in Poland
by Amazon Fulfillment
Poland Sp. z o.o., Wrocław

91046020R00080